Koestler Voices: New Poetry from Prisons, Vol.1

With a foreword by Benjamin Zephaniah
Edited by Kate Potts

First published in the UK in 2017
by The Koestler Trust, 168A Du Cane Road,
Shepherd's Bush, London W12 0TX.

ISBN 978-0-9574101-8-3

Design by Polimekanos

Koestler Voices: New Poetry from Prisons

With a foreword by Benjamin Zephaniah
Edited by Kate Potts

Inside

Outside

Portraits / Pictures

Letters / Confessions

Introduction

The Koestler Trust was of course founded by a writer, and so it is fitting that we should be bringing the poetry produced by our award-winning poets more to the fore than we have done previously.

In 2016 the reaction of our UK exhibition visitors to the poetry curated by Benjamin Zephaniah in his Speakers' Corner section of the show was overwhelming, and, for the first time, a poem was chosen as a recipient of our Audience Choice Award in our exhibition at mac in Birmingham. So our audiences were also our inspiration.

Koestler Voices Vol.1 marks our intention to produce an anthology biennially to celebrate, enjoy and reflect on new poetry from prisons.

I would like to thank all those who have made this possible: our poets themselves, who will all receive a copy, as will every prison library; the Koestler staff, in particular Fiona Curran, Nathalie Bristow, Mali Clements and Laura Pattison; the T. S. Eliot Foundation for its early and enthusiastic support; all our Crowdfunders who brought it to fruition; and our editor, Kate Potts, without whom it could not have happened at all.

Sally Taylor,
Chief Executive

Foreword

Welcome to *Koestler Voices: New Poetry from Prisons*. Welcome because when you engage with this publication you are not simply reading a collection of poems, you are going places.

In 2016 I had the pleasure of curating the Koestler Trust UK exhibition, and I gave a lot of space to poetry. I even created a kind of Speakers' Corner, where visitors could stand and deliver their own poetry. I want to give voice to everyone. I just love poetry, and, although it might seem politically incorrect to say, I love prison poetry, it's true. I know that if you are writing poetry in prison you have to think deeply, you have to use your imagination, you have to go for a ride.

These poems are absurd and strange, they are light and heavy, they are intense, intellectual, and playful. They are honest.

I have the greatest respect for everyone at Koestler. I've seen how passionate they are about prompting creativity from behind the walls and showing it to the world. And I have a great respect for the women or men who for whatever reason have found themselves on the wrong side of the wall, but have still found time to express themselves. Having said that, when you read these poems, forget about Koestler, forget about the walls, and go where the poems take you. They are just poems, written by human beings. They just happen to be really, really good poems.

Benjamin Zephaniah

Inside

Nightingale at Dartmoor Prison

The nightingale begins the night's ritual
And lands with exuberant notes as gift
On my window ledge, to take my victuals.
I close my eyes and bathe in beauty's lift.
Her song is drowsy and meandering
Like summer days or streams without an end
And though she's gone while I am wondering
She's wooed me so's I scarcely comprehend.
Though now is dusk she returns before dawn
To sing her solo on a silent stage
So wows my heart and mind, leaves me reborn
And washes off for now this place's rage.
    Exquisite bird of love, my love is true
    Ever a home is here; ever for you.

Solomon

The Visit Hall Beckons

the visit hall beckons
familiar faces
conjure up images
of freedom.
one hour of dad's infectious laughter
the weans are runnin riot,
mair interested in sweets.
mum asks, 'how you doin?'
ah tell her, 'ah'm fine.'
'Yer brother came hame drunk', she says
'he'll end up in here wi you.'

Anonymous

A is for...

ALCATRAZ
ATTICA
ADX
ANGOLA
AUSCHWITZ
ABU GHRAIB
BANGKOK HILTON
BANG KWANG
BARLINNIE
BROADMOOR
BELMARSH
BELSEN
CARANDIRU
CAMP-13/22
COLDITZ
DARTMOOR
DACHAU
DEVIL'S ISLAND
DIYARBAKIR
EXETER
FOLSOM
GUANTANAMO BAY
GULAG
HOLLOWAY
ISIS
JAGALA
KILMAINHAM
KONYO
LONG KESH
LA SANTE
MAZE
NEWGATE

OAKLAND
PARKHURST
PELICAN BAY
PENTONVILLE
POLLSMOOR
QUINTE DETENTION CENTRE
RIKERS ISLAND
ROBBEN ISLAND
SAN PEDRO
SING SING
SAN QUENTIN
STRANGEWAYS
TADMOR
TREBLINKA
USK
VIRU
VANTAA
WORMWOOD SCRUBS
X-RAY
YAMAGUCHI
Z-CAMP
ZYKLON B

Nicholas

Networked Gym-Fit Recidivist

This is what I've learnt from being
    in prison again.
I've learnt five out of us 750 have three weeks
    to sew a creatively written patch.
I've learnt it pays to be first in the queue
    for the servery or go hungry.
I've learnt the sound of nonchalant callousness is
    a prison officer bellowing.
I've learnt that gym or chapel makes us feel
    less like income-streams or cattle.
I've learnt your best source of help is your peers
    so I'm networked. And gym-fit.
I've learnt how to make a tattoo gun out of a
    PlayStation Two.
I've learnt most murderers look like me, or you.
I've learnt of a Joint Enterprise robbing you blind.
Care UK, Carillion and People Plus; they're on
the inside.
I've learnt that the Immigration Service's delays
mean foreign nationals have extended stays.
Oh, and by the way, taxpayer
you're the one who pays.
I've learnt a part-privatised probation worker has
    eighty or ninety on her books
And will recall us on a whim, depending on
    how her in-tray looks.
I've learnt a paranoid schizophrenic's sojourn
    was nine years beyond his sentence
And he'll now trade coffee or food for a burn.
I've learnt the Juno team's ineptness
    makes them carpet-bomb all domestics.

I've learnt a broken-legged Vietnamese was
      untreated for sixteen days.
I've learnt a man from Vilnius
      pulled out four of his own teeth.
I've learnt that a towel and a kettle is all
      you need
On healthcare wing, under constant obs
      for a suicide to succeed.
I've learnt that prison is a Mecca for the shopper.
'Burn', Spice, prescription meds, narcotics of any flavour,
      mobile phones of any colour.
I've learnt that despite private profit's prison glass
      there's neither rehabilitation nor correction
with many street-homeless post-detention.
It's just a scam, the wrapper's off.

Neil

IF

A prisoner's perspective
with apologies to Rudyard Kipling

If you can sleep in bed while tannoys beckon
A long and seemingly endless list of names,
Keep a strong, tight hold on your possessions
Whilst others try to win them with mind games...
If you can stay out of other people's business
And ensure others stay out of your own,
Think 'It could be worse, in some ways we are lucky'
Whilst everyone around you wants to moan...
If you can cope with having no say in decisions,
Nod and smile, although you don't agree,
In your room, display your chapel calendar
And not mark off the days until you're free...
If you can put up with clothing going missing,
And wearing the same shoes daily on your feet,
Gulp down heaps of potato, rice and pasta,
Feel blessed to find a single chunk of meat.
If you can watch friends leave and not be saddened,
Knowing that it will be your time soon,
Return to your room and dance around wildly
To the latest over-played pop tune...
If you can keep your head held high
Through all your times of hardship
And leave, a stronger person in the end...
Then this is your cell and everything that's in it,
And what's more you can do prison, my friend.

Michelle

Whales

From my cell widow
I see the long curves of the Downs,
like great whales
stranded on the unseen shore,
the rising of their great chalk bulk
built from millions of skeletons,
white beneath the green skin of grass.

Then on TV I see breaking news –
on the coast, upon another shore,
a family of fabulous creatures
like pictures from an old story:
whales, stranded like refugees,
helpless victims of our tides
with a one-way ticket to oblivion.

Anonymous

Sonnet for a Cretan Tree
(Zelkova Abelicea)

Outside my window there's a foreign tree,
Each morning it's the first thing that I see.
I often wonder how it came to stand
Upon this very piece of no-man's land.
Those who planned the prison let it grow,
And built this place around it years ago.
The RHS have blessed it with a plaque.

But does it ever dream of going back,
Across the years, the miles, across the sea?
Does it long for friends and family?
Although its leaves dance on this English air,
Does it yearn to blossom over there?

It has no choice. It is a refugee.
My fellow prisoner, the migrant tree.

Stephen

The House of Pain and Mending

In the house of pain and mending
stands a long table in the kitchen
where food and rage is chopped and swallowed.

There is a new baked cake
iced with grief.
Take a slice for everyone.

In the house of pain and mending
furniture and fabrics hiss and groan
with secret hurts whispered pummelled
yelled communicated through the skin.

In the house of pain and mending
perhaps the mending like a tailor's
is invisible unlike the pain that screams
its presence like paint too bright upon a wall.

Nigel

Therapy

Iced lakes and withered branches
Chilled feet and numb ears
Are signs of summer's end.

Men walk backwards through time
In search of yesterday,
Yet, to no avail, find
Yesterday has fallen
Like the leaves of autumn.

Truth is on the stove
To warm bitter bones
That are as cold
As primeval thrones.

Tears defrost and fall,
Burning through masks
That are icy sharp,
As therapy thaws
Arctic hearts.

Moses

McFly

('Readin' in the Seg…')

I caught a fly!?
– as I was reading?
– *wrapped* in the silence
that only a SEG can bring?
– Quite by chance? Quite by fluke!?
– Between those pages of my booke!?

Trapped, my fly stared out at me
– and I, in turn, at it…
but you see I Despise flies now…
– they fly back an forth
– and forth an back
– between me – an my slop bucket
d e l i b e r a t e
(to remind me ov the smell)
– and I wonder…
am I still as gentle an kind
I was once so proud to be…?
You see, I Suddenly wanted to Squish my fly
S l o w l y
D e l i b e r a t e
– N*ot* by chance, N*ot* by fluke
'tween those pages
…ov my booke
Cruel in fact…

– and in doin' so I found
after *juss* 4 (*years*) underground...
that I must have after all,
...turned another page...

Tony

Lock Down

Let me lie upon the
ground
and place my hand on the
mound
of that sweet remembered earth
to feel the sun warm my
skin
and watch the ants go
wandering
lost among fine hairs
that are no true
barrier
for they each could
carry their
weight, faint as a dream.

Let my fingers dig
deep
and the soil will anchor me in
sleep
yet awake, but far away
where she now
dwells
in a memory that
tells
the past that I am here
waiting for her to
sit
beside me and kiss where the ants
bit
the redness pressed by her lips.

Let her laugh at my
ouch
as we rest upon the gentle
couch
of warm grass in a summer gone
then we turn onto our
backs
to look at clouds built into
stacks
of creamy pudding high
or mashed potato, she
says
with a smile that
plays
with my heart.

Let me stay another
moment
in the past that will always
torment
me with its loss
in the dream where she
lives
holding my hand and
gives
me still her heart
as if to a faithful
lover
but the alarm wakes me with yet
another
lockdown.

Bob

Inside

Inside the iridescent iris of lucidity
Cinema of sleep, both panoramic and microscopic
Stippled light, nowhere but omnipresent.

Lights, hues, noise indeterminate
Flashlight, blinding, then lightning.
Now dusk of dreaming, the other realm.

Fantastical landscapes, colours alien
Yet familiar, mirrored leaves
Reflecting opaque lakes.

Denser than water, imploding sea,
Waves, flesh petals on human flowers,
Silence deafening, then listening
In animal frequencies, sonar and ultrasonic
Whales and bats, then the alarm clock, outside now.

Anonymous

Dirty Laundry

We all arrive soiled, some more than others,
the source of lost pride for so many fathers and mothers.
The wash programme selected by the judge and jury;
But so often injustice – the cause of much fury.

Locked inside the drum, the cycle begins,
The theory is simple – to wash away sins.
Clean once more, the rinse cycle starts.
Time has been served, a cleansing of hearts.

Freshly laundered, the washing is aired.
Inside for so long, many are scared.
The final task; it is time for pressing.
Iron out the creases, the fresh start is a blessing.

Tim

PRISON YARDS

AND COLD DESPAIR

AS WATCHING GUARDS

AND INMATES STARE

AT CHEVRONED GEESE

WHICH FLIT AT WILL

NEED NO RELEASE

TO FLEE THE CHILL

WINTER DARK

FREEZING NIGHTS

SO THEY EMBARK

ON AWESOME FLIGHTS

I PRAY THEY WILL

ALL REAPPEAR

COZ I WILL STILL

BE WATCH

Christopher

N

LONG AWAY

OFF THEY ROAM

COMES THE DAY

TO MAKE FOR HOME

OFF THEY START

CANNOT WAIT

CALLS THEIR HEART

TO FIND A MATE

WITHOUT REST

CROSS THE SEA

BUILD A NEST

AND PARENT BE

I KNOW THEY WILL

RETURN EACH YEAR

BUT I WILL STILL

NG HERE

Succession

a street corner angel
still tasting violation
squeezes a floor splinter
out of her knee

sunshine shone
through the window casting
a shadow of bars
unto his appeal papers

Leslie

Outside

Killie Bus Tales

(The Number 11)

Ah'm sittin upstairs oan the number eleven.
Ther's four neds behind me – two men, two wumin
drinkin cans a Super n Frosty Jacks
(ah wish ah hudnae sat sa close tae the back).
The men – in identical trackies, trainers n hair
ur bad-mouthin mates who urnae ther
n squeezin the cans tae get aw the dregs
n moanin aboot the queues in the chemist n Greggs.
The wimin are talkin about due dates n lib dates
n the've crumbs oan their chin frae yesterday's steak beaks.
Wan's visitin her man who's in the jail
the dad's his best mate who's oot oan bail
(Nothin tae worry aboot fur a while
then it'll aw get sorted oot... oan Jeremy Kyle).
Ther's a commotion noo comin up the stair
some guy wae a baseball cap n his burd wae red hair,
him in Crosshatch, Voi n fake Stone Island,
her cerryin 6 carrier bags fae Farmfoods n Iceland,
eyes hawf closed n skin colourt leggings
fu'a the blues n Gappapentin.
Tho' her haunds are full n she's in some state
she still manages a mouthfa of her Frijji milk shake
as she barks oot the order 'Mk me a roll up Steven'
n a voice fae behind shouts
'here mate, yer burd looks like Ed Sheeran!'

Graham

Time Dragging

Switch on the TV, **BBC** Breakfast,
zero six thirty, time for a coffee.
Three and a half hours, am I going to last?
Shakes then start up, wish they'd leave me be.

I sip on coffee wishing it was booze,
sweat runs down by brow, I feel hot and cold:
I should not drink but I've nothing to lose;
make another coffee – God, I feel old.

Two hours pass but it feels more like four,
why does it seem my clock is in reverse?
Not long to go now, can't take anymore;
I will get what I need then be on my erse.

Head out to the shops in search of a cure,
I glug it down. Getting better? For sure.

Anonymous

Jesus Green Lock

Liquid silk
The river
Folds over
The weir
Angular shear
Sliced off-cuts
Gather pace
Rushing to
Another place

Antony

empty chair

empty chair, warmth of sun
cold beer, the clink of ice in mum's spiced rum
barbeque smoke mixing with skunk
tapping of feet to *Fool's Gold Funk*
children laugh splashing without a care
daisies and bluebells in their hair

but no one mentions that empty chair

Graham

Thirteen-0-Clock

Concrete canopies,
Unwanted monoliths,
Deprive oxygen to the masses.
Gasping heads, with computer chip eyes, despise
Their poisonous superiors with corrupt technology.
Walking cameras neutralise
Paper thin resistance,
Pulp factions.

Brick bastions,
Bullying tower blocks,
Anesthetise sunlight into electricity.
Contented smiles are gagged and double crossed
Bleached faces, with crocodile teeth and tears,
Watch the funeral skies and their neighbours.
Drones squish any attempt
At individuality
Or a backbone.

Mother Nature,
Flowers and dirt faces,
Replaced by flat-back convenience.
Contented smiles are stopped and double crossed
By agencies, that stomps on acts of self-indulgence
Blind obedience required
By a large relative,
Big Brother!

Anonymous

I Built a Rocket Ship

When I was a little boy
Part of the Human Race
I built a rocket ship
And flew it into Space
I flew it to the Moon
And then on to planet Mars
Then I just kept on going
Heading for the stars

I flew it up to Jupiter
Saturn and Uranus too
I flew it up to Neptune
Where everything is blue
And then I left the Solar System
Just kept on going straight
On into the Universe
Supper would have to wait

I flew on through the galaxy
And into the boundless night
Into the never-ending
And beyond the cosmic light
I saw black holes and quasars
Supernovae as well
Things that looked like Heaven
And some that looked like Hell

And when I'd gone far enough
Seen all there was to see
I turned my ship around
And headed home for tea

But back on Earth, my beautiful Earth
I'd been away so long
Everything had changed you see
Everyone had gone

I built a rocket ship
And flew into Space
The last remaining person
The last of the Human Race

Jonathan

We Will Find Solace

We will find solace
here in this moment
among our friends
in creativity and invention
in the rhythms
of the tide

We will find solace
in the wildness
of places
in the rumbling stones
on the soaring hills

We will find solace
by the meadowed fields
by whispering streams
north by northwest
beside the stone-shod lake.

Phillip

Animal School

Kangoraffe swung from the minibus.
The tikey sat in the trees
Mank hog danced round the granddads
And dolanroo fell to his knees.
The octolope lay down on the grass
Antodile ate all the flowers
And Elepus dug up the car park
Hedgebat has sat in the traffic for
Hours and hours and hours.
Girphin slid through the ice cream
Crocphat climbed on the gates
Womger drank from the toilets
And every one was late!

Jacinda

Selkie

Meet me on the beach
I'll shed my tears for you
Save your coat for me

Tease the married heart
a selkie you can't resist
trapped by just one kiss

Once you find a coat keep it
close and hold it tight
a partner for life

Selkie temptation
can't resist the grey seal's eye
moonlight love and die

If you were a selkie
would you shed your skin for me
or drag me to the sea?

Anonymous

The Widow and the Children

Deep in a forest, living harmlessly
A vulnerable widow was distressed
By two unthinking children (H and G)
Who vandalised her cottage for a jest.
She felt for them – the mites were thin as rakes –
So took them in and fed them bread and milk.
They devoured the biscuits she had baked
Then went to sleep in sheets as smooth as silk.

When morning came, the widow wished (of course)
To bake the children bread for a present
But in her fiery oven she was forced
By youngsters with a murderous intent.

You parents, telling stories, making dreams:
A fairy tale may not be all it seems.

Anonymous

See nothing, hear nothing, speak nothing

One evening, late, I crossed the street
to miss the accusing eyes of men
in smart uniforms and shining boots red
with the blood of men at their feet
I looked at the pavement, examined my shoes
and I saw nothing.

One morning, early, I turned up the noise
of my radio, to drown out the screams
that smart uniforms and shiny boots
could tear from the lungs of my neighbour's sons
I read my paper, listened to the news
and I heard nothing.

One fine afternoon, I held my head
and tasted my blood and wept my tears
while smart uniforms and shiny boots
dragged and kicked and took me away
where no one will hear and no one will see
and now, I am nothing.

Anonymous

Eviction Day

A pair of rain-wearied Nikes
A pink soft toy, muddied
A teething ring
A blue and brown sweater
A bargain store tea-set
A duvet, stained and soaking,
Detritus of a life surrendered
Dumped in a roadside heap
When the locks were changed

Take only what you can carry
Pack the year into boxes
The bailiffs' appointment is fixed.
Go sit with your kids
At the HPU
We'll sift through the wreckage
See if there's anything
We can use or sell
From the things you've left behind.

Clean bricks hide dirty money.
We're all Rachman's children now
Digging out new basements
To bury the homeless deep.

Four left-foot shoes
a ballet flat,
A black Adidas
A workboot,
A kid's slipper
School text books

And a Post Office statement
A bundle of post
A hospital letter.

See if the shop has some spare boxes,
Try and borrow a neighbour's van.

Sleep in a park
Sleep in a car
Bin-diving for survival
Under bridges, under bushes,
Freezing White Lightning and Lyrica nights.

Clean bricks hide dirty money.
We're all Hoogstraten's children now.
Buy-to-rent, buy off-plan,
Dying for a home.

Nick

Never Again?

According to the news

'If the body had landed a few metres either side,
it would have landed on a busy roundabout or near
a row of shops.'

To fall from the sky
While chasing a dream

To fail in the chase
When the dream is a lie

Minus 60c
Clinging to the undercarriage of a plane
A 12-hour flight
Dead or half dead by the time you dropped

And bodies floating always in the Med
In the Aegean
Bodies meeting borders
Bodies meeting barbed wire, tear gas, stun grenades

Aleppo burns
Homs burns
Mass graves in Sinjar
A farmer in Burundi says 'We are sick of people dying
    like goats.'

Militarise
Criminalise
Exclude

'We have got to break the business model of
    the criminal smugglers.'
The always-already-ever-convenient European
    mea culpa
Slicing and dicing the universal
We are close to the edge of that 'Never again'
That repeats and repeats
While barbed wire, rifle butts and tv cameras
Improvise ghettos
And we drag children from trailer containers
To hold them in freight sheds
While fat white men who hide money overseas
Talk of 'one in, one out' and 'fast-track returns'
And place a holding camp between the words
    'human' and 'rights.'

Nick

The Sun Did Not Rise

The Sun did not rise this morning, and I waited
    for hours.
A clear blue haze stretched from horizon to horizon,
the air remained cold, frost did not melt.
By midday I gave up and went home.

The news said the Sun had not been seen since yesterday.
Nobody knew what to do.
So they sent out search parties.
Evening came; it did not feel so strange,
but I went to bed early anyway.
Sunshine can not abandon you at night.

I went back to the same hill in the morning,
there were loads of people waiting.
It was very quiet, electric, filled with gnawing
    anticipation.
Everyone stared wide eyed at each other;
    hoping, expecting.
Birds flew down and sat on our shoulders, watching us!
As if we knew what to do!
Rabbits and squirrels and foxes stood next to us,
as we all emptied hope towards the dim haze on
    the horizon.
And then the rains fell like tears from heaven,
washing our hopes away.

A stranger turned to me and whispered,
'If our hearts are warm, will that not do?'
I thought for a moment and replied,
'Perhaps we just need to stand closer together.'

Alan

Portraits / Pictures

The Piano Player

hooch fuelled
male voices
full of angry
jobless depression
rumble like
distance thunder
in a dingy shebeen
where smoked
starved
light and liberty

the piano player
strolled sex
over ebony and ivory
his fingers knew
highs and lows
of down and out days
when sound
was all there was
between
lust and loneliness

Anonymous

The Field

There has been no rain.
A sheet, shades of grey clouds, loom high,
covering the landscape.
Below the clouds an empty sky is still.

Distant snow-capped peaks of the mountainous backbone
divide known from unknown.
In the partly harvested field
a framed, fossilised, track of a machine.

The rustic earth, rolled out like a carpet
covering a lonely space.
Ghostly trees line the far perimeter.
Their trunks, like terracotta sentries, divide.
Branches become twigs, reaching out,
and up, collecting moisture from the air.

Opposite: row upon row of an unknown crop.
Slender, green, leaves unfold for attention,
others droop, like the ears of an alert Dachshund.

Beside a small hole a lone figure stands.
A shovel shares his weight.
His close-cut hair a shade
of the grey clouds above.
His face is solemn, head bowed.
His wrinkled skin, buttoned up shirt,
trousers short, as if expecting a flood.
He blends with the colour of the earth.
Beside him,
shrouded in white swaddling,
an infant. Lies still.

                                        Anonymous

Guiltfoot Ron

Ron's got a foot made completely of guilt,
No muscle or bone in his heel or his toes,
It's just the way he's built.

He's got an angry knee
and an eyeful of fear,
An ambivalent thigh,
And a strangely complacent ear.
The left one, the right one's intense,
One elbow's for real, the other's all pretence.
He's a wistful smile and an anguished wrist,
His sternum's sober but his ribs are half-pished,
He has two clinically depressed fingers
And one very glum thumb,
His shoulder blades are emotionally numb.

But the thing that really sets Ronnie apart,
And makes him the sum of his complicated parts,
Is his compassionate, generous heart.

Tom

Dys-Leg-Sarah

Words squirming like wriggly squiggly worms on a page
Squiggling and reforming in a mass o' rage
Ah cannae read them as thay move aboot
Ah know ma alphabet withoot a doot

Thay skirl in fancy dances, whirling in strange patterns
Some wear mocking smiles n grin like tumshie lanterns
Thay float n jump, inrun helter skelter tae hide
Bit the wirst are them tha oan ithers dae ride

Ah thocht a wiz stoopit no bein abilt tae read
Noo ah ken thit am disabilt an noa a deid heid
DYS-LEG-SARAH tha's what a think it is
Wurds dinnae form frae le'ers, it's aw jist fizz

Am no youngster wi rose colirt glesses
You'd think Ah was Elton John or some wee lassie
I've tried them oan n thay work fine n dandy
Faur lang ago thay wid've been gie handy

Thay wurds arnae wurms ony mare
Thay dinnae like ma spellin' – wha cares?
Ah kin write and read a book
So stoap gein' me yon funny look

Anonymous

Susan's Bosoms

We take the D-bus from
St Andrew's school

Susan shows me her
bosoms in the back of the bus
and tells me I'll have them
soon

I'm not entirely sure
I want them

they don't seem to be much good
for anything

She says they're for feeding
babies

I say 'Why don't you just give them
a sandwich?'

Heather

Cheeky Boy

I'm told our little old dog has died:
He was rescued when I was put inside.
As all of my girls were off living away
He was rescued by the good old RSPCA.

They re-housed him (that must have been a job
For a pop-eyed runt with a yappy gob).
Nah, he looked good really. Well, handsome (nearly)
And all the family loved him dearly.

He'd his gold tan coat and sharp little face,
A fine specimen of the canine race,
And his USP, one which never did pale
Was his proud, flowing, magnificent tail.

I hear he's been happy these two last years
But hope someone learnt to fondle his ears
as he lay on their chest to gaze in their eyes
With the love of a dog ten times his size,

Let him sit for a while upon their lap
Snuffling and snorting as he had his nap.
Chasing cats in his dreams (which all got away,
He's do just as bad the following day).

I hope: he never missed me, didn't cry.
But when at last our Cheeky Boy did die,
In his heart, or in that little doggy brain,
a small memory of me did remain.

Richard

Baggy Skinned Tangerine

Gifted a tangerine
the size of a fat orange
plump dimples presaging
juicy tumescent sacs
an inviting nipple of peel –
motherly not loverly –
offers itself as the gateway.

The less than gifted, gifter
waits, expectant eyes
eager to vicariously consume
the exotic prandial pleasure –
emotional onanism
masquerading as altruism.

The pliant peel
willingly succumbs to
impatient digits sliding between
firm, but supple
fruit purses and velvety pith.

As luscious skin is shed
loose gaps between pipless portions
selflessly present themselves
for immolation: evolution, designed
for reproduction, de-engineered
for impotent consumerism.

The giftee
carefully separates the eight
segments, laying them

as a smiling face on a
1968 Penguin edition of *Nausea*.

The gifter
ogles this dismemberment
and post a shameful
pre-prandial completion
nods and walks away
satiated but empty.

Mark

Black Tree

Birds nestled into
hollow shoulder of death, tree
ask for no applause

James

My Wales

When I think of Wales off-peak...
it's of white folk that don't speak –
well at least not English
and gather in pubs to stare at me, mum
and my white auntie Linda...
Never seen a negro? I won't point the finger.
Caravans that lean worryingly towards the sea,
gave moi Titanic nightmares
and made a 'land lubber' of me.
Shops...
stuffed to the rafters with very little shelving –
had me spinning around looking for treats –
like a Cyclops.
A beach so forbidding...
no sand just pebbles and rubbish
and rocks...
A sea so gluey and grey, you'd be a buffoon –
to jump into, for what all intent and purpose...
was a monolithic spittoon.

When I think of Wales off-peak...
it's of me mum's knitted tops
and welly bobs
and endless afternoons in teashops,
forced hikes, like Royal Marine types
and a chemical toilet that look like it bites.
Summarised by Atlantic gales –
that leave the Atlantic to batter Welsh vales,
half open fun fairs, where the land met the sea,
it would be 'fing' freezing,

and no one could feel anything by the time we were
    leaving...
my Wales.

Anonymous

Glesga Jesus

I wance met Jesus in Glesga,
Hunkered in a doorway, doon the west end,
Can o'Carlsberg in is haun.

Aroon him, shoaps, coppers 'n' dugs,
Awe dain their miserable business,
He wis dain his.

Wae a haun as black as a tenement,
He wiped his ocular mooth,
Growling his simple teachins.

'Sod em all, sod em all!'
'Lost the lot, lost the lot'
'Guid riddance, guid riddance.'

He watched me as ah passed, the nothing ah wis,
In that inelegant Scottish half lotus,
The void of the afternoon,
The void in his eyes...

He watches me still, crouched in the doorway of ma mind.

David

Letters / Confessions

Where I Sit

When the unfairness of the storm
Gathers about you
And blankets you overhead
Pitifully
Pouring its rain upon your closed doors

You should light the fire

That burns the logs
Which summons the warmth
That melts the pain
And the fright that fogs

Boil the kettle
And write me a letter
A note
That tells me of your present plight

We paddle the same craft
Of aloneness, you and I
Caring, keeping us afloat
Ruffled waters

Binding us together

It's a fair distance
To where I sit
Huddled between grey walls
Lit by windows of refracted light
Tortured
By wondering how you are.

Phillip

I Know How Judas Felt

I know how Judas felt.
He wanted Jesus all to himself.
When that didn't happen,
and the five men
Matthew, Mark, Luke, John
and THE ROCK Peter
were getting preferential treatment.
It really upset him

What was Jesus's problem?
Hadn't he dropped everything
to follow the Messiah?
Admittedly he'd taken time
to change his substantial
bank account into travellers cheques
at a decent exchange rate too.
These were now stuffed
down the front
of his designer boxers,
hidden from straying eyes.
A thought had occurred to him
that the all seeing Jesus
may be aware of this transgression,
but dismissed it as too fantastic.
So there was Judas
on the periphery of this holy gang,
worrying about his empty
unguarded house.
His girlfriend
who he hadn't told
he was leaving,

Just in case
This son of god thing didn't work out.
As the weeks went by
NOT ONE WORD OF ENCOURAGEMENT.

It became intolerable.
He'd show them.

Anonymous

Sacred Silk

i,

What became of you?
Do you still conceal in
Sumptuous silk and satin the
Number, which hallmarks your wrist?

Do you still hide the past
In ornate trinkets? You vowed
One day we would dissect in
Our own little dust storm.

Was this the reason you
Left? If so you must return,
I understand. I now to
Bear a number.

ii,

No time to waste.
Make haste, gather your
Trinkets, discard your sacred
 Silk, dare to live.

I am eager to forgive
In the midst of our own little dust storm.

Warren

Raining Pain/Reign in Pain

You poured abuse on me,
        a substance you hoped would corrode.
            It is my mortar.
You rained your fists on me,
        endless thumps you hoped would break me.
            They are now my bricks.
And I've built the walls around me.
        I built a castle from your crumbs.
I've been locked away for too long,
        Silent and numb, scrabbling in dirt
            To build a castle from your crumbs.

Each belittling you hurled
        was just words you hoped would scar me.
            They've become my doors.
Each rape you forced on me
        was safety that you hoped to steal.
            They're my iron bolts.
And I've locked the door before me.
        I built a castle from your crumbs.

You hoped that your touch would destroy.
        I'm no longer your little girl,
            I built a castle from your crumbs.

Your beatings now are beating drums.
        Your abuse, my bricks and mortar,
            Solid doors, iron bolts
With your crumbs you couldn't break me,
        I built a castle from those crumbs
            And I'm ready to reign.

Anonymous

When you find where I live...

'When you find where I live
will you love me enough?'
he asked.

Years passed without a
visitor, no polite conversation,
tea time chat.

Where I lived shifted;
Love shifts, I know that.

Anonymous

Understand Me

Understand me disposing of the past, though it
bears your name it has no relevance.

Understand me eating all the food at 2am,
in the morning I will regurgitate the sun.

Understand me locking the door at midnight,
throwing the key away. Later I will climb in
through a window.

Understand me painting your toenails while
you sleep, in the morning's confusion there
are alligators under the bed.

Understand me exchanging your water
for a typewriter, if you wake up thirsty
in the dark you can tap me out some
words of suffering.

Understand me forgetting sonnets under
floorboards, when they creak in your
slumber you'll feel me beside you.

Understand breaking into swimming pools, climbing
trees and eating birds' eggs, chasing foxes over rooftops.

Understand me arresting the terrorisms of the night,
over breakfast I'll let them loose in the kitchen.

Understand me not cleaning my boots of their
excursions; I'm not stealing chickens. In your
heart a suspect is hiding.

Understand me burying the roadkills of the day,
the act has no significance except you are not
aware of it.

Leon

Two Toothbrushes

Somehow it's those little things,
The here and now
A mind content,
And a heart
which sings.
Two toothbrushes
Share one cup in a bathroom,
One with soft
One with hard bristles,
Both fairly worn
With usage
Their mileage
Time's testament
To whatever kind
Of marriage.
Tokens of togetherness
Two toothbrushes
No more or less
A kind of bliss,
Let's keep it like this.

Paul

Grandfather Clock

You kept my heart under a stone brother,
almost like it meant something.
A thousand tiny fireflies in a jar brother,
unquiet spirits
on the tangled path from childhood.

I'll fight you for the grandfather clock
that stood sentry through our sleepless nights.
I matched you tick for tock then brother,
swing for swing
even as the minutes ate the silence.

Under cover of covers we listened,
to the poltergeist smash the plates
to father slamming the door,
and to the tearful ghost
creeping up the stairs
to bed.

Anonymous

If You Want to Know Me

If you want to know me
Examine with a collector's eye
This old, blue bag filled with ancient coins,
Found in the dusty attic
Of my father's childhood home.

This is who I am.
Once cleaned to a shine, grey becomes gold,
Like fragments of history, revealing secrets of the past.
This is what I am.

Jason

The Koestler Trust

The Koestler Trust (charity no. 1105759) is the UK's best-known prison arts charity. Since 1962, the Trust has inspired ex-offenders, secure patients and detainees to take part in the arts, work for achievement, and transform their lives. The annual Koestler Awards receive over 7,000 entries across 51 artforms, such as poetry, film, sculpture, music and drawing. Professionals in each field volunteer to judge the Awards and write personal feedback to the entrants. Entrants gain certificates and feedback and can win awards, apply for mentoring and showcase their work. Recent Koestler Trust exhibitions, including displays of written work and performances, include *Inside*, in 2017, curated by Antony Gormley, and *We Are All Human*, in 2016, curated by Benjamin Zephaniah.

Each year the Koestler Awards generate over 1,000 poems – making poetry one of the most popular categories. Recent poetry judges include Bidisha, Mark Waldron, and Sarah Howe. *Koestler Voices* provides a sample of this engaging and unique writing by serving prisoners, and ex-prisoners in the community and secure hospitals.

The Koestler Trust is grateful to the selected poets, all those who took part in the 2016 and 2017 Koestler Awards, and the people who supported and encouraged them to do so.

Supporters & Acknowledgements

175 people supported our first crowdfunding campaign to make this anthology happen.

We are very thankful to:
Ian Acheson, Aku, Eve Aldridge, David Andrew, Annie, Jeffrey Archer, Geoff Ashman, Rosemary Ashton, John Ashton, Andrew Auster, Peter Baker, Roger Barberis, Diana Barnes, Ruta Beadle, Jack Beaton, Alan Bennett, Elizabeth Benoit, Kathy Biggar, Barbara Birch, Helen Boothman, Paul Borlase, Nicholas Bowlby, Paula Bowles, Linda Bright, Nathalie Bristow, Mary Brodrick, Edward Brooke-Hitching, Gill Brown, Ross Bull, Andrew Burford, Jenny Callan, Philippa Cardale, Beatrice Charles, Zelda Cheatle, Alexandra Citron, Shaun Clarke, Beth Crosland, Fay Curtin, Manos Daskalou, Bill Davies, Oliver Davis, Mary Davis, Stephanie Donaldson, Maya Donelan, Drawing Connections, Sandy Dutczak, Emma, Kate Finney, Kate Fish, Frances Flaxington, Isabella Forshall, Elizabeth Marie Fox, Phoebe Gardiner, Cara Garven, Patrick George, Katherine Grainger, Emma Hammond, Rosemary Harley, Tanya Petra Harris, Matt Harris (in memory of John McGrath), Lewis Herlitz, Fi Hibbs, Sally Hiscock, Matthew Hobbs, Jacky Holliman, Sarah Holyfield, John Howkins, Sarah Humphreys, Kitty Hunter Blair, Sally Hurcomb, Mel James, Jane, Camilla Jessel Panufnik, Peter Kaye, Jenny Keen, Susan Kellas, David Kendall, Janet Kerr, Amy Key, Jane King, Basia Korzeniowska, Andrzej Korzeniowski, Helen Krarup, Sophie Lancaster, Martin Langford, John Lawlor, Mark Lehane, Paul Crane & Gerard Lemos, Sarah Leonard, Janet Lewis, Htein Lin, Niamh Linnane, Margaret Lipsey, Jackie Littlechild, Chloe Lund, Heather Macvie-Martorana, Harry Man, Alastair McGann, Clare McGowan, Jane McKenzie, Fran McLean, Sian Meader, Jill Miller, Caro Millington, Sandra Monks, Madelaine Moore, Helen Morris, Mary Murphy, John Myers, John & Serena Naismith, Anja Nurkkala, Stephen O'Donnell, Mulika Ojikutu Harnett, Katy Parkes, Heather Pattison, Frances Peebles, Rebecca Perry, Alexandra Phillips, Theo Pigott, John Plummer, Peter Price, Jennifer Pullan, Joyce Quarrie, Stuart & Nami Ralph, Deb Rindl, Rosemary Rinn, Sylvia Roberts, Tim Robertson, Nina Robinson, Mark Rogers, Sally Rogers, Fern Roy, Kirsten Sams, Sandy & Tim, Rachel Shackleton, Zoe Shapiro, Annie Siraut, Janet Smith, Anne Smith, Tanya Smith, Graham Smyth, Jessica Southgate, Richard Spencer, Caroline Starling, Judith Stocks, Keir Stone, Stuart Stone, Angela Swan Greaves, Robert Taylor, Vilyana Tsekova, Rick Tucker, Unilink, Sally Varah, Caroline Walker, Tony Walsh, Russell Webster, Kirstin White, Anthony & Martha Whittome, Tania Wickham, Rob Williams, Kate Wilson, Christine Wong JP, James Wood QC, Erica Wood, Wendy Woolf, Andrew Wright, Jane Yeomans, Lynda Young Spiro, Carola Zogolovitch, and to all those who wish to remain anonymous.

Also, huge thanks to:
Susan Aldworth, Clare Argar, Polly Astor, Shaun Attwood, Jane Beese, Grace Bridger, Julian Chichester, Owen Clarke, Lee Cutter, Rishi Dastidar, Tim Dooley, Claire Dyer, Nicky Hessenberg, Melissa Hoffman, Rachael Horsley, Sarah Howe, Rachel Kelly, Ellen Kirkhope, Sabrina Mahfouz, Bidisha, Femi Martin, Raheel Mohammed, Geoff Nunn, Adam O'Riordan, Rachel Piercey, Gill Saunders, Louise Shelley, Ruth Sykes, Alexis Taylor, Jack Underwood, Mark Waldron, Carole Warburton, Emily Wood, Caroline Woodley, Tom Woolner and Benjamin Zephaniah.